All our grandfathers are ghosts.
Pasha Malla

All our grandfathers are ghosts.

Pasha Malla

Hi Herb –

No murders or bloody
gore in here, but this
one's pretty weird, I gotta
warn ya.

Thanks again,

Snare Books . Montreal . 2008

Edited by Alessandro Porco
Designed by Jon Paul Fiorentino
Copyedited by Marisa Grizenko
Typeset in Gill Sans and Adobe Garamond
Cover Art by Balint Zsako. untitled (black roots) 2008

Library and Archives Canada Cataloguing in Publication

Malla, Pasha, 1978-
    All our grandfathers are ghosts / Pasha Malla.
Poems.
ISBN 978-0-9739438-8-7
    I. Title.

PS8626.A449A64 2008   C811'.6   C2008-904788-5
Printed and bound in Canada
Represented in Canada by the Literary Press Group
Distributed by LitDistCo
SNARE BOOKS
4832 A Avenue Du Parc
Montreal QC
H2V 4E6
snarebooks.wordpress.com

Snare Books gratefully acknowledges the financial support of the
Canada Council for the Arts.

Canada Council   Conseil des Arts
for the Arts   du Canada

Contents

1. We wore our nametags home.

The Proper Grammar

I suppose a gun shop wasn't the best place
to stop to buy *gum*,
even if you did misread the sign,
Harold.

But when the guy behind the counter
showed us that .22,
like a discovery of unfamiliar briefs in the hamper,
things changed.

"This'll crack a kneecap like a pecan,"
he told us, cocking
the thing that you cock.

When you asked,
"How much?"
I wondered if you'd forgotten
about the $80 entry fee
to the hot dog eating contest,
and that we'd pooled
all our laundry money
for months.

How soiled my trousers were
— and yours, too, Harold —
that day
in Manitoba.

Goddammit, sometimes
I wish my wife
weren't so in love with you.
I wouldn't do these things.
I wouldn't find myself driving

off the highway onto dirt roads,
jiggling over potholes
with a gun on your lap,
trying to find somewhere quiet
to pull in so you could
shoot me in the head
like a dog.

But who shot who
in whose head, Harold?
Who shot *whom*,
whatever.

The men named James and the woman, Alice

There are the men named James.
There is also the woman,
Alice, who once was "late"
and decided to get an abortion,
but then discovered she wasn't
pregnant, not at all.
Since then
she's given up meat.

Every day, one of the men named James
goes to watch the penguins. This
he finds soothing.
Another of the men named James
is a terrific masturbator.
Another is not named James
but goes by "James"
due to his uncanny resemblance
to the Hollywood movie actor
James Cagney. (Or is it James Carrey? Or
is it James Carrey doing Jimmy "James" Stewart?)
Another James is under house arrest
for stealing a dolphin
from the local marine biologist,
James.
Although he's not such a factor,
not so much. Neither is the marine biologist James, either.

There are other men
named James, also.
But none of them
has any distinguishing characteristics.
They are all just muscles and beard,
muscles and beard.

There is a man named Gregor
who lives down the street
in a tarpaper shack
and who raises goats for sale
to Jamaican restaurants,
but this isn't about him.
This is about the men named James
and the woman, Alice.
That's it.

And there's no time for romance, what with
Alice too busy practicing archery
to even think about
getting involved with any
– let alone all –
of the men named James.

Alice is not a slut.

Yeah, they just live together
in a commune
sponsored by the microwave popcorn
barons, Redenbacher:
the men named James,
the woman, Alice,
Mr. (James) Roper, the superintendent,
and his wife
who has Lupus
and for whom everyone feels
an almost incapacitating sadness,

although nobody knows her name.

Best Poem Ever

This is for the poor shepherds. I am a communist.

– Allen Ginsberg

A friend of mine won that contest
for Best Poem Ever
and she won't shut up about it.
You'd think she'd won
the Oscar
for Being Awesome,
or something,
when really all she got was
sixty dollars and a plaque
donated by Starbucks.

The truth is
that the poem isn't even that good.
I mean, it's probably better
than this one.

After the ceremony
in the lobby of the Holiday Inn
they interviewed her on Global News
and she glared into the camera
like a real asshole
and told everyone watching,
"This is only the beginning."

Before, she was pretty cool.
We'd hang out, get Dairy Queen,
listen to CCR and sometimes just drive
out into the country,
not knowing where we were going,

just us and the road and the night and the time
glowing green from the dash.

Now, though, she's a different person,
this friend of mine.
When she goes out in public
she wears sunglasses and a big hat
and ignores anyone who talks to her
in case they're
jonesing for an autograph —
even the handicapped,
even the lost.

She sighs a lot.
She complains
about what's on the radio,
flipping endlessly from station to station.
Once she even faxed me at work
to say she wished she'd
never been born.
But I guess this is what that guy
slinging luggage at the Greyhound station meant
when he said, "¿La poesía, mi hermano?
A poetry
can change your fucking life."

Booty Call

My friend Steve
got this booty call the other day:
"You have a. Collect call. From:
Fuck me."
After he accepted the charges
Steve said, "Hello?"
and the lady on the end of the line
said, "Laser?"
and Steve said, "Laser here,"
and things haven't been
the same ever since.

Steve makes me call him
"Laser," now, see,
mainly because after that night
he turned into a Laser.
You know the type:
one of those guys
who'll take his shirt off at the park
and can throw a Frisbee
like a ventriloquist –
that is, into the distance,
and trickily.

Laser came over this morning blaring
New Rock from the Alpine system in his
brand new Pontiac Sunfire.
I barely recognized him.
"You've changed, man,"
I told him on the way to
my mom's sentencing.
"Whatevs, brah,"
he said. "Whatevs."

That's the other thing:
Laser calls everyone "brah,"
now, and when the valet at the courthouse
came to park his car he
just started dry humping the air
in the parking lot,
moaning, "That's it, baby,
that's it,"
and pumping and pumping
and pumping and pumping.

Who's Josh?

At the symphony,
I was amazed to discover that
the entire orchestra was playing
the same song.
Not one bassoonist or trumpet-guy
had succumbed to the urge
to bust into something different.
The conductor flapped his arms
and everyone blew or strummed
or struck and at the end
the crowd rose, clapping —
all of us, at the same time,
even me.

Then I went home
with Andrea, the one with the horse posters
all over her apartment, and the horse magnets and horse figurines
and horse bedspread and horse-decorated dinnerware,
and the horse nightlight glowing golden over the toilet.
We did it to Enya
on her futon, like always.
Except:
"Josh!" cried Andrea.
I stopped mid-swirl.
"Who's Josh?"
"Josh?"
"Josh."

Josh,
of course,
was the name of the horse
her father had gunned down
in their backyard when Andrea
was small.

In the movie adaptation of *The Godfather*
a man awakens to a horse's head
in bed with him: "Khartoum"
was this horse's name.
The following morning,
after the symphony,
Andrea awoke to a live horse
tethered to the armoire, neighing,
and which I had stolen
under cover of night
from the local butcher, a Frenchman.

Sometimes, love
is like picking up
and holding to each ear
a cat
and listening for the music
of the seas.

Five Very Short Poems about America

But I wonder, David,
do you think
you could get me
a job
at the orphanage
where your parents
left you?

*

You've never been
to Lake Michigan?
It's great.
It's a great
lake.

*

Take
those boots
off.
You're tracking AIDS
all over
the damn house.

*

I don't know
any Latin —
but
I sure love
the music.

*

And remember, kids:
Karate can kill people,
so be real careful
who you use
these moves on.

Money for Nothing

A guy Stan vaguely recognized
from high school
showed up at Stan's house the other day.
He's a banker now, or something with money, and works
on a street
the name of which connotes guys who wear
those white-rimmed glasses the guys in eyeglasses
ads wear.

Stan was out on the lawn
under a partly-cloudy October sky
raking leaves for stuffing into a
community quilt about Hope,
thinking without nostalgia
of his car, the keys to which his ex-girlfriend's father had handed
over
on his deathbed
and which Stan had just sold for parts, when
this guy came steaming up the driveway
with a look like someone
who'd just been told the lottery
had been won by a person
with cancer who was also a retarded person,
or whatever,
and said,
"Hey, Malinsky!"

This was interesting.

Stan's last name was not Malinsky.
A certain Malinsky
had been a classmate of Stan's,
back in school,

and a look-a-like for Stan's
grade ten best friend —
his twin brother,
Malinsky.

"Alright, Malinsky," said the guy. "You
listen and you listen good.
I am going to drop a fifty-dollar bill
on your mother-
fucking driveway.
And then I am going to take a
goddamn shit
on top of that there
money.
And if you want that fucker —
Malinsky!"

Stan had been focusing
on the spittle
spraying
from the guy's mouth;
at the corners was foam.

"Are you listening, Malinsky?
Are you even listening?
Do you hear what I'm saying
to you, right here in the middle of
your son-of-a-bitchin' driveway
standing here on God's green earth?"

Stan told him yes.

"Alright, Malinsky,
you want that money,
you can pull it out of my fresh
hot turd.

Are you ready? Are you
ready for this, Malinsky?"

And then the guy's pants were down
and he was squatting —
all in one motion,
it was quite fantastic.
"Steal from me?" said the guy. "Rip off my firm, will you?
Malinsky! Look at me!
Now I'm taking a shit right in front
of your rent-subsidized house,
and you're just standing there!
Who's the asshole now, Malinsky?
Who's getting fucked two ways to sideways?
Malinsky!"

He howled and
pooped. The poop
descended like a fainting sea urchin
and folded itself into
a neat little pile.
In his eyes was triumph.

But where would he wipe?

Stan could tell the guy was wondering the same thing
squatting there with his silk trousers
at his knees.
He looked like someone who'd called in
sick to work and bumped into his boss
in a House of Mirrors.

Stan sensed his chance.
"What about the fifty?" he demanded.
"What?" said the guy
who thought Stan was Malinsky.

He straightened and did up his pants.
"You said you were going to drop a fifty-dollar bill
on my driveway," said Stan, "and shit on it.
I see the shit.
Where's the fifty?"

The guy's hand went to the pocket of his blazer,
where rich people keep their wallets.
Holding it there he looked
at what he had produced on the driveway
and he looked
at Stan, and he looked
back at his own shit,
which steamed in the cool autumn air.
From somewhere close came a rumble
of thunder.

"Did you forget who you were dealing with?" said Stan.
"I'm Malinsky, my friend. Not just anyone.
I'm the man who stole
from your firm, right under your nose. I've
made a joke out of your entire operation."
He put his hand out.
"Now
pay up."

Something in the guy's eyes sparked.

"So it is you!" He came striding forward
with confidence renewed.
"For a minute there… right after…
I wasn't sure. But now you've
admitted it!"

He stood on Stan's lawn, maybe
a foot away.

What
he'd left on the driveway
Stan could smell now;
it was all Stan could smell
and it smelled of
diseased rats
who subsisted only
on all-you-can-eat
Indian buffets.

"Alright, Malinsky, you're on!" screamed the guy,
and reached into his blazer.
A fifty-dollar bill came out
like magic. It was the colour of Ferraris.
"You want my money?
I shit money bigger than you.
I. Shit. Money,
Malinsky, you piece of welfare-getting ass.
What do you shit? Huh?"

Stan made a
tell-me-see-if-I-care
gesture.

"Shit, Malinsky.
And all you'll ever
shit is shit."
He shook the bill.
"You want this here fifty? You want it, Malinsky?"
He squatted again,
just as niftily as before.
"Then you can go — " he hiked his sleeve "— and get it."
And plunged the money
Rolex-deep
into his poop.

For a minute here
things for Stan go sort of blurry.
All he remembers is being suddenly
alone.

The clouds were gathering fast
and a wasp
was investigating
the feces on the driveway —
taking it for fruit, maybe,
or something with which
to build a nest.
Thunder sounded again,
above and slightly to the east.

From the guy's turd
a corner of the fifty poked out,
just enough to pinch between one's
fingernails, probably,
and extricate.
However,
despite being in what they call
financial woes
for some time —
mainly due to a series of poor decisions
regarding that professional debate league
a bunch of us had tried to get going
in the mid-'90s —
even Stan had his limits.

But Stan was nothing
if not resourceful.
He went into the garage and got the
tinfoil sort of thing
that acted as a wind-blocker
for his camping stove.

This, breathing
through his mouth,
Stan duct-taped in a circle around
the turd on the driveway,
leaving a small gap
for drainage.

Pride is one thing,
but Stan was in
dire straits, and this was money for nothing.
When the rain came, he figured,
the shit would wash away
but the bill would be trapped
inside its new metallic home.
And come the rain would,
soon,
as clouds Photoshopped the sky grey
and the air
settled into the
promise of a storm.

Stan finished stuffing the Hope quilt,
went inside and
washed up.
When he came out again,
with the quilt packed inside
a waterproof carry-all by the Glad company,
the first few raindrops had begun to fall.
The turd on the driveway was already
melting into a brown stream.
The corner of the fifty wavered slightly
in the breeze.

Under his arm
Stan tucked the bundled-up quilt,
lovingly patched with squares

designed by the children and recent
immigrants of our tight-knit community,
and took it
over to Malinsky's house,
where Stan laid it out
on his living room floor,
rolled on a condom
and, laying down with her on top of it,
made sweet, gentle love to Malinksy's wife,
Rachel.

II. Challenging popular ideas of mediocrity.

I got my MFA in haiku and this was my thesis:

One, two, three, four, five.
One, two, three, four, five, six, sev-
en. Shit, I fucked up.

Baseball: A Cricketer's Primer

The Game
The object of baseball, like cricket, is for the team at-bat to score runs by whacking a ball with a bat away from the defending team. Unlike cricket, chewing tobacco figures heavily. Also unlike cricket, the rules of baseball stipulate that the ball must only be whacked forward, into a predetermined area. Forward, onward, upward! Such is America.

A standard game of baseball is structured into nine innings in which each team is afforded an opportunity to bat. This is only fair. Otherwise, there would likely be complaining and possibly tears.

The team at bat is allowed three "outs" before they must don their leather mitts and swap places with the boys in the field. Outing in baseball is an uncomfortable situation for every man involved — there is much shuffling of feet, and then a sheepish return to the dugout and the consolation of sympathetic comrades. "I, too, have been outed," they will say, patting their broken teammate's buttocks in a supportive fashion.

The Uniform
Imagine the clean-cut, poster-worthy good looks of a cricketer. Now, add a moustache: baseball.

The baseball uniform consists largely of that stirrupped trouser popularized by the television show Fame — the same trouser championed by yoga enthusiasts, soccer moms and eight-year-old ballerinas across North America. There is also a shirt, which bears the name and number of each participant, lest he misplace his clothing in one of baseball's infamous pre-game nude team frolics about the "clubhouse."

Despite there being little chance of ever mixing up players, the home team in baseball is usually dressed in white, while the visitors appear in something darker. Admittedly, this color co-ordination is often stunning, and even the least fashion-savvy baseball fan will delight in the numerous costume changes and extravagantly designed stirrupped trousers showcased during a baseball game.

Governance

Baseball is governed by a team of angry white men dressed as elementary school custodians. They call themselves "umpires." An umpire's authority stems from the Proustian reaction to his outfit by the players, whose memories of childhood reprimands for lofting another utility ball onto the school roof surface painfully with every at-bat.

An umpire is a grumpy creature, surliness being a pre-requisite. As is a barrel-like chest, Conservative-leaning politics, a diet of ribs and Coors Light, a policeman's haircut and the black patent leather shoes of a small-town mayoral candidate.

One of the favorite activities of any umpire is hollering accompanied by the pumping of fists. The particularly dignified will only pump. The umpire delights in the outing of players: "You're out!" he will holler, and then watch gleefully as the fellow slinks off to the dugout and the eagerly awaiting palms of his colleagues.

The Field

Instead of the fragile beauty of a wicket, the baseball field of play is anchored by something called a "plate" fashioned in the manner of children's depictions of houses. This is intermittently dusted off by the umpire-cum-custodian, who will bend over in a provocative fashion and waggle his posterior at the hundreds of fans in attendance, waggle and dust, dust and waggle, like a French maid or an obsessive compulsive chimpanzee in heat.

When things are satisfactorily clean, the umpire will straighten up and announce saucily, "Now there's a plate you can eat off of, boys."

While the cricket pitch is a simple rectangle cut delicately into an oval, baseball opts instead for a diamond with a strange tumor-like growth blooming out of it called the outfield. The outfield is where a great deal of outing takes place, hence its name. A pop-fly into the outfield is an especially glorious occasion; all in attendance will be on the edge of their seats, anxiously watching the ball arc up into the stratosphere. "Will there be another out-ing, Daddy?" demands a small boy of his father. But Daddy is steely-eyed, stroking his moustache, following the path of the baseball up, up, knowing full well what might just happen. Once, long ago, before the ACL tear, he was being outed, too.

At times a batter will have some luck, and a ball hit into the out-field will not be caught, and he will not be outed. Occasionally, a batter will smack the ball clear out of the park, at which point he is allowed to trot freely around the bases like the clever pony he is.

Sestina to Save the World (draft #964)

I give up.
I give up.
I give up.
I give up.
I give up.
I give up.

Etc.

Explaining Novelty T-Shirts to my Mom

"I'm With Stupid"

See how there's an arrow pointing to the side? The thing underneath "Stupid"? The arrow? Yeah, I know there's no one there. But you're supposed to — no, no, it doesn't matter that there's no one there right now. Just imagine — okay, pretend he's with someone, then. It doesn't matter who! Honestly, Mom, it doesn't matter. Anyone. Okay, sure, Tom Selleck, then. No, he's not suggesting Tom Selleck is stupid. Oh, I totally agree. One of the best shows of the 80s. Yeah, for sure. Ummm… Rick, I think? And the black guy was called TC. I don't know. Tom Courtenay, maybe? I honestly have no idea. Oh, I never thought of that, Mom. You think so? You really think Higgins was Robin Masters? Yeah, I suppose that would make sense.

"I'm not as think as you drunk I am"

So you know when you get drunk, and — whoa, whoa. No! Of course not! That's not what I'm saying! Mom, Mom — listen. Yes. I know, I know. Three years is a long time, and we're all very proud of you.

"Krap"

You're familiar with Kraft, right? The food company? Good. Yeah, so they took the logo from Kraft, and made it into Krap. See how it's the same, sort of? Yeah, yeah, yeah. What do you mean? It's funny because the company's called Kraft, and they made it Krap. Like they took a popular brand name, and made it into a swear word. Yeah, sure, I think you can say crap on TV. It's not a big deal. Yeah, they used to say bitch on NYPD Blue all the time. Oh, I don't know about that one — maybe only in Canada. Yeah, they're tougher on that stuff down there. What's that? Mom, I can't hear you. Stop whispering, I can't — Mom! Easy! Easy with the blue language, we're not — oh, no, that lady over there is looking at us. Don't look now! Mother. Please. This is the worst. This is the absolute worst, ever.

"I found Jesus — He was behind the couch the whole time"
Okay. I know you're not religious. But you are aware, are you
not, that there are people who — figuratively — "find Jesus."
What? Oh, those are quotation marks. It's like, you do the quo-
tation marks sign with your fingers when something's figurative,
or ironic, or whatever. God, Mom, I have no idea. Just go with
it, okay? Listen — can we start again? Good. Thank-you. So
there are certain Christian people who — no. Okay, I've got it.
When a Christian person really gets in touch with God, they
claim they've found Jesus. And sometimes they ask other people,
"Have you found Jesus?" What now, Mom? What? No! You
don't do the quotation marks thing when you quote somebody,
not when you're talking. I have no idea! You just don't. Well,
maybe you don't make very much sense, either.

"Beaver Patrol"
Hey, look, a shoe sale! You love shoe sales!

"Gary Coleman for Governor of California"
Okay, this one is ironic. Like, it's sort of making fun of Gary
Coleman. Yeah, from Diff'rent Strokes. No, that was Webster.
Some disease where they look like kids all their lives, or some-
thing. Well, I think their life expectancy is limited, so maybe
not. Stick with the wrinkle cream and pilates, Mom. Okay.
Now, the t-shirt. I think he actually did run for Governor, and if
people voted for him it was probably a joke. I don't know what
his platforms were. Well, because he's a former TV star, and he's
small, and on Diff'rent Strokes he always used to say — yeah,
right. Jeez, Mom, you actually do that really well. So I guess it
would have been funny. What? Yeah, last year. Hmmm…I
don't know. I never saw any. Although maybe that is how
Schwarzenegger got in.

"Firemen Always Have Big Hoses"

Why are you giggling? It's not even funny. Mom. Seriously. It's a lame joke. It's so easy — "Firemen Always Have Big Hoses". I mean, come on. What? Oh, I don't know. Are you serious? I just don't do that sort of stuff — big penis humor. I wouldn't even know where to start. Oh, good one. I'll write that down. I don't even think policemen's guns are that big, to be quite honest. Mailmen? Mom, no one finds mailmen sexy. Don't. I know what you're thinking, but don't. Oh, God. Mom! If I ever thought I'd hear my mother say "Big Sacks". What? The quotation marks? I had to do them that time. I don't want you putting words in my mouth.

Ghazal for Allah

Nah,
just kidding.

The Fancy Traveler's Guide to the Glory of Europe

Spain

If it is the summer, wear Rayban sunglasses. The Spaniards will marvel at their own beauty in the mirrored lenses. Everywhere, there will be bulls. You may at some point find yourself fleeing a herd of them. If this is the case, you should scream, "Olé!" except with an upside-down exclamation mark before the O. This will be exciting: you could well be hoisted onto the shoulders of strangers, or else crushed mercilessly and left battered and dying in the streets. Olé means "bull" in Spanish.

France

In France you will find that the men dress like women, while the women dress like Cossacks. This is purely coincidence. The baguettes are delicious. You must go up the Eiffel Tower: there will be children in berets on bicycles. Nothing anyone says to you will, at any time, be comprehensible. At some point pretend to forget where you are and order French Fries in a restaurant. This will result in incomparable hilarity.

Czechoslovakia

Czechoslovakia has disappeared. No one can explain this.

Italy

If you do not enjoy spaghetti or organized crime, do not go to Italy. The national animal is the boot. The pope can be found here, gloating. Beware also the village of Pisa and its shoddily constructed buildings. The graffiti artists in Italy are heralded as geniuses. The boots are shaped like Ireland.

China

China is just outside of Europe. You will have to take a bus to get there. In China you will find more people than anywhere else in the world. There are literally millions and millions of Chinese people — it can boggle the mind. Especially your mind, because it is so feeble.

Romania
Romania is the smallest country in the world. No one has ever even heard of it before. The people here will seem eerily silent. The newspapers are blank: you open them up and there is just empty page after empty page. Through your entire visit, what you will never realize is that Romanians communicate through a complicated series of eyebrow movements, and that Fred Savage is their king.

Ireland
All of Ireland is green. Everyone sings, always. There are many Catholics, and many more redheads, and still even more Irish people. Often you will find yourself in rollicking, hilarious situations. Begrudge the Irish for this. They are only laughing at you.

Holland
In Holland your family will be delighted to discover the following: tulips, windmills and whores. All three are highly recommended, preferably in conjunction. The people in Holland will speak English, but poorly. You will find this frustrating, and may be stricken by uncontrollable fits of rage. Luckily there are many beautiful vistas. Holland is widely considered among the sixty best countries in the world.

Sweden and Turkey
Sweden and Turkey are mortal enemies, and as such, should be avoided. The Swedes are cunning and deceitful, while the Turks are notorious curmudgeons. If you do find yourself in either Sweden or Turkey, take as many photographs as you can, for they will be your last.

West Germany/East Germany

You will be able to tell the different sides of Germany by the color of denim. In the West, it will be red. In the East, it will be black. Blue jeans are strictly forbidden. Germans, both Western and Eastern, are avid historians — ask any German what their country was up to in the 1930s and they will be happy to tell you. Visit Germany in October, unless you are some make of pansy.

Switzerland

Switzerland is a country of mountains and knives. There is also a brand of cheese shot through with bullets. If cornered by a rabble of drunken Swiss in some alpine chalet, do not panic. They are only trying to get to know you. Also of note is the incorrigible Swiss appetite for pornography. Children should be sequestered at all times, but by no means alone with a Swiss babysitter. Pray to God you are never so foolish.

Portugal

Of all the countries in Europe, Portugal is among them.

Poland

Poland invented the colour maroon, and its people pride themselves on this. Go ahead, ask any Pole. They will explain it all to you. Do not be frightened. The Polish can sense your fear, and it stimulates them.

England

On any visit to Europe, England should be the last place you visit. And by this I mean that only out of utter desperation should you even consider stepping foot on English shores. Here the cattle put their hooves in each other's mouths. The fauxhawk is the official hairstyle for men. If for some reason you cannot avoid England, it is best to remain in your hotel room, sobbing, occasionally ordering a delicious scone from room service.

III

All our grandfathers are ghosts.

Natalie Portman, Listen

I

Natalie Portman,
listen:
they say the pen
is mightier than the sword,
but I'm inclined to believe that
if I showed up at your mansion
and held a two-foot-long saber
to your throat
and said, "Marry me,"
it would achieve a lot more
than these few feeble words.

But we're getting off on the wrong foot,
and I don't even own a sword.

Natalie,
I just want to get off with you.
I want to kiss you
all over your body
but mostly
between your legs
where the vagina part is.
Or not even.
I would be happy to only kiss your mouth,
slow or fast, or medium,
depending how it is
you like to be kissed —
I would do that, totally.
Although
I will certainly take sex
if that is also going to be available.

I don't even care
that the only good movie
you've ever been in is
The Professional and you are like thirteen
and not even hot yet —
at least not legally.
All the others have sucked.
See how strong my love is? I am willing
to overlook everything about you
except how pretty you are.

I wish someone would make a movie about you
the old way,
in which beautiful women were without apology
objectified by the camera —
but with reverence.
I think even Eve Sedgwick
would put down her dukes for a moment
and just watch.
There would be so many soft-focus
close-ups of your face
looking off-
screen with your mouth
parted slightly and your eyelids
half-lidded and the world
would sigh a little bit at each one.

II

I need to admit something:
the only Jewish wedding I ever went to
I showed up late.
They'd run out of yarmulkes.
It was in a hotel.
I hadn't brought a date; I hadn't
been allowed. I'm not very tall and they had me
seated next to a woman who seemed
at least twice my height.
So when it came time to dance,
I didn't.

What I'm trying to get at
is that your body is a synagogue,
Natalie,
and I would purchase and wear a yarmulke
if you chose to let me in.
I would come on time.
I would dance a saucy Semitic dance.
I would recite from the Torah —
all your favourite parts —
if it would help.
Or none if that would be preferable.

Fuck, Natalie,
what do you want from me?
I'm tired of guessing.
This isn't a relationship,
not what we have.
A relationship
is about communication
and I feel like I'm hollering
into a tin can
attached by string
to a Star of David made of restraining orders.

III

Natalie Portman,
all I hope
is that this poem makes you come over to my house.
I wouldn't even
have to be there.
You could just breeze through
and when I returned home
it would be a game to see if you'd
left your scent on my furniture
or a pee in my toilet.
I would never flush it down.

I want you inside me,
Natalie. Be my Valentine.

If for any reason you cried a river of tears
I would be happy to drown in it
or at least flounder for a while,
waving intermittently at you on the shore. Or
I would kill
an animal for you;
I would kill a wolf or bear.
Or I would save an endangered bear
from poachers
and kill them instead.
Or kill no one,
just run through the fields of some alpine
location with you with the breeze in our hair
and the bears and wolves and poachers
cavorting around us,
and violins.

We could just hold one another
on a bearskin rug

by a fireplace on fire, Natalie,
at your mansion.
There would be jazz, Natalie, and wine,
and if we started to take our shirts off
the camera would pull respectfully away
up over the white leather couch,
across the room,
past the portrait I had painted of you, Natalie,
in my extremely awesome loft-style artist's studio
on Manhattan Island, New York,
where I know you also live, Natalie,
and I would be living casually at the time,
and then the camera would turn out the window
to the night, Natalie, and the stars, Natalie Portman,
and start to zoom and zoom
and the Foley guys would be doing
love sounds while we started
dryly humping, sly
as teens and soon
the only thing on-screen would be
the big white amazing moon.

Who's Schtupping Bubbie?

I went to visit my Bubbie
in the old age facility the other day,
and on the way home I realized,
My god!
I don't think I'll ever
get enough of
that business at the zoo
when animals of opposing species
fall in love:
a leopard suckling a lemur,
a baby elephant
tucked into the pocket of a kangaroo.

Sometimes one is an orphan;
sometimes it is because of
loneliness, sometimes camaraderie; sometimes
some twisted zookeeper has just
stuck them in a cage together
and laced the water supply
with E.

In the wild they would be enemies.
They would tear one another to shreds
with their talons
or be a parable for children.
But at the zoo there they are
holding one another as close
as gays to Streisand.

San Diego has the best zoo!
The worst being in the next town over.
Think of San Diego
as Noah's Ark with refreshment stands,

the other as a bestiary of the damned
where no one wants to see some shitty lion cub
being groped by a half-blind ape,
not when over in San Diego
an ostrich is striding about
with a litter of adorable piglets saddled up on its back.
And, in San Diego, the ostrich can talk.
And it is wise; it is succinct.
It says things like, "Patience" and "Believe."
The ostrich says, "Forgive,"
and the ostrich says, "Forget."

Who's schtupping Bubbie?
I believe it's the Lebanese guy
down the hall.

What I Want in a Newscast

In a news anchor I want
someone who'll
ask the tough questions.
Like, "Does a bear eat people
and think, *Delicious?*"
and then cut away
to someone at the mall
being mauled by a grizzly.

I want to see some beards; no one ever has a beard.

When they go to commercial
I'd like to have
an inkling that something's afoot
in the studio.
And when they're back it'd be nice
to see some scuttling.

The reporters' voices
are always a sine wave of quarter notes
lilting up and down the same octave.
I'd enjoy some
impressions.
How about "Crazy Italian Pizzeria Owner"?
All you need to do is add an A
to the end of every third word.
Or "Deaf Person," or "Bruce Lee,"
or "Gay."

More gays —
but I mean *really* gay.
Like they're wearing
leather chaps and

just raping
all the other guys in the studio, all the time,
pretty much always.

The women I'd rather
were doing that thing with a knife
where you stab it between
the fingers of your outstretched hand,
quickly,
with a look of focused, resolute
madness in the eyes.

The weathermen would broadcast
the weather onto their own naked chests
painted bluescreen blue
and the lightning would be real lightning,
striking them in the nipples and sending smoke
sizzling out their ears.
If it were raining they would turn
the sprinkler system on.
For tsunamis they would have to improvise.

The sports-guys wouldn't feel the need
to yell the sports; they'd tell it
in a reverential whisper.

Maybe instead of sitting behind a desk everyone
should be sprinting through a field —
of landmines.
Or instead of a studio they'd
be treading water in a shark tank,
also featuring landmines.
Instead of suits everyone would be dressed
in tattered loincloths and
instead of make-up
their faces would be streaked

with the blood of reporters from rival networks
they'd vanquished in battle
and instead of just cameras doing the shooting
they'd occasionally be shot at with guns.

I just want the broadcast
to match what they're reporting.
No more cutting back
from a hospital full of limbless children
to a studio done up with bunnies and tinselly baskets
for Easter. No more
following genocide with witty banter
about the local high school
football championships.
No more saying the word, "Doozy,"
ever.

I want mayhem.
When on the other side of the world
a village is flattened by bombs or nature
and dozens of moms are wailing on their knees
in the rubble-strewn streets,
I want the news-team to weep; I want
to see them wring their hands and collapse
and I want to hear them
wonder, "Why, why, why?"
And I want them to look deep into the lens of the camera
with tears running down their face
and I want them to feel like no one's watching
and I want them
to ask me, "Why?"

Emmanuel Lewis Is Dead

Not really, not yet.
Although you'd assume so,
wouldn't you?

But consider:
if I were to write down the words,
Emmanuel Lewis is dead,
and I waited long enough,
they would eventually be true.

And maybe the same could be said of anything.

God is dead.

And so is Emmanuel Lewis
and so am I,
motherfucker,
and so are you.

A Very Horny Normandy

Lazlo and all the other
people from his Sex Addicts
Anonymous group were conga-
ing, fine, along
the beach,
when all of a sudden they
stopped.
The guy behind him, Jerry,
started kneading Lazlo's shoulders.
Lazlo scanned the group
and realized that despite
the steel-band doing their damndest,
everyone was massaging
whoever was ahead of them
and the back of the line
began looping around
so Cybil at the front standing
there with her hands out like a strangler
had someone to rub.

After ten years of marriage,
Lazlo and his wife Maureen
had recently divorced.
He'd gotten in the settlement
a ferret named Sol
and the bicycle built for two
Lazlo himself had constructed for their ninth wedding
anniversary and which Maureen
had never deigned to even mount.

God, Lazlo loved
to fuck.

Or so he claimed.
Fact is, he'd given up
on sex;
he just figured signing up for the group
was a good way to meet people,
now that he was single
and sole owner of that bike and all.
Maybe he would find someone to
ride it with him, he figured – someone
with a good sense of teamwork,
which was important in a marriage
or a partnership of any kind.
As was not bonking
the pool guy
or the cable gal
or anyone who came to the door
with pamphlets or a clipboard,
or a beating fucking heart.

But almost everyone, it turned out, was couples.
At the first meeting
they'd all stood up in pairs
and holding hands said their first names
and admitted, in chorus, "We are sex addicts."
When it was Lazlo's turn
he had to assume people were
thinking, "With whom?"
and that also he was a liar.
But everyone had been supportive;
"Welcome, Lazlo," they had said
at the leader's urging, Mike.

Every week Mike would sit the group
down in a circle in the back room
at the Transportation Museum and over
Peak Freans and Sanka

get them to talk
about lapses in celibacy,
which would cure their problems,
claimed Mike. "Be strong," he told them.
"Say, 'I will not,' and then don't!"

They went around.
You could pass
and Lazlo, never anything but celibate, usually did.
But, wow, the stories! Better than porn!
Lazlo soon found he was going home
and touching himself to many of them –
the lesbians Lily and Franka's
sordid tale of finger-banging in the baking aisle
at the grocery store, especially.
"We couldn't help ourselves," explained Lily.
Franka nodded guiltily,
and Lazlo crossed his legs
and later hammered off for all he was worth.
Afterward, shameful, Lazlo
started wondering if he shouldn't join
a different group.

Oh, but there was one woman,
Bev, who showed up alone like Lazlo
and never had much to say.
When things came around to Bev
she shook her head quickly
and turned to the person beside her
and when they started talking she'd nibble a Peak Frean and
gaze off at the replica of the
Avro Arrow suspended on cables
from the museum's ceiling.

Bev wore a cardigan and Reeboks.
She took the bus

and one of these days Lazlo was going
to work up the nerve to offer her
the spare seat on his bike, definitely.
Although he was conscious that she assumed
he was a sex-addicted pervert
like everyone else, so
it was risky.

Anyway, here they were: Cancun.
Mike had suggested a retreat
as a reward for everyone's hard work
all autumn.
On the flight
Lazlo sat between Mike and Bev
and casually, he thought, offered
them each a Certs at take-off and landing.

Despite the all-inclusive package
Mike advised that perhaps one drink each
that first night
was a smart idea.
He himself had just gone to the bar
as the conga business got going
with the sea rippling silver
under a pretty good moon.

Things started okay.
Everyone found their place and the band
began and the line shuffled along,
a giant, Hawaiian-shirted centipede
kicking sand along the beach.

But, quickly,
it all went to shit.
Maybe it was just the touch of flesh
on flesh, but yearning took hold

and soon the line closed
to form a circle.
The steel-band stopped playing.
Shirts came off
and one by one, bodies began to fall to the sand.
It was like Normandy, in a way –
a very horny Normandy,
and everyone was Nazis.

Mike appeared holding a coconut with a straw
and an umbrella sticking out of it, which he dropped,
screaming, "This is supposed to be a conga line,
not a daisy chain!"
By then the entire group was writhing
around, naked and orgiastic – except for Lazlo,
who stood in the moonlight, a pillar of salt-
y restraint.
But where was Bev?

There was Bev,
God,
there she was:

bathed in moonlight
with the surf
washing up around her,
hissing like a secret.

Geena Davis:

Is being a genius like
being high all the time?
Like being high at a party
where you're the only one
who's high, or
it's you and maybe one or two pals,
high, and you sit together
on the couch
watching a guy barf into a plant
while his buddy rubs his back,
telepathically communing,
"So many morons,
so many goddamn morons."

Stop Following Me

Himself he devises too for company. Leave it at that.

– Samuel Beckett

I

Stop following me,
says the fortune inside the fortune
cookie – and you think,
"Fuck." You think,
"How
does the cookie know?"

II

Imagine working at a school with a girl
who is six,
autistic
and a genius.
Her name is Zoë: life.
When you try to convince her
to join the other kids gluing buttons and fluff
to paper plates
she turns for a moment away from the sonnet she is writing
and explains:
"Art isn't art
if it has to be taught."

Later you find yourself
in a bar in a conversation
about art

61

with people so cultured they pronounce the p
in excerpt and don't even find
farts funny anymore.
Even when one
mentions "the ontology of postmodern experience,"
you keep quiet, nod,
considering the chicken thighs
defrosting at home on your kitchen counter,
and how long once thawed
before the salmonella kicks in?

You're not ignorant, you don't think –
just resistant.
You're aware, for example, of the evils
of egg-farming and milk,
but imagine free-range to be worse:
a sort of barnyard Lord of the Flies
with the heads of farmers skewered on stakes,
the mad hoots of insurgent roosters
heralding the dawn at noon,
at dusk.

III

Imagine that you and a friend
go to play tennis on a warm day in October,
the trees already leafless and bare,
and when you get to the court
they've taken the nets down
("they" meaning those men
who putter around the city in pick-up trucks
with their drive-thru coffees and moustaches,
parking wherever they please).
You decide to play anyway
and although you commit to a policy of honesty

neither of you double-faults once
and you've never hit your backhand so well and true.

This friend, this same friend,
you took a philosophy course with in university
where the only question on the final exam
was: What is the difference between a tree and a poem?
You wrote something about bark
and got a D.

Back then, see,
you were going around with a cheerleader-type –
literally a cheerleader, on the team
and everything.
You'd go to watch her
get thrown around by men
without necks.
The sport required them to grope
her hips and buttocks, apparently,
put their hands up her skirt
and fling her at the ceiling,
catch her by the waist and lower her gently
on the way down
and then stand wide-legged and clap.
You watched from the grandstand with popcorn
in your lap and clapped.

IV

Imagine that you move to a different city.
On the subway
you take to taking
in a stranger's face
from across the car
and then looking away,

trying to hold onto the image of them, whoever they are,
for as long as you can.
Usually it's four stops
before the mouth starts to fade,
the nose collapses,
the eyes become two holes burnt through smoke.
The worst was when you look up
and the person is gone,
and you can't check to see if what you remember is right.

Cleaning out your pockets
in this new city,
you discover a pen
from somewhere you've never been.
Turning it over in your hands
you try to figure out where you might have picked it up.
Maybe part of you left for the day,
floated up over the city and touched down
at "Jack's Auto Body Repair"
ducked inside
and surreptitiously pocketed things
from around the waiting room.

Remember when the whole family
took your grandmother mini-golfing
before she died? It was your mom's idea.
After nine holes
you decided to pack it in,
your sister in the lead by six strokes, you
in a respectable third.
At home in her purse Granny discovered
the little yellow pencil used to keep score
and made you return it.
The girl behind the counter
looked bewildered:
the pencil lying diagonally across your palm.

like a gift from a toddler
offered up to a bemused houseguest.

V

When you talk to people with accents,
like an asshole,
you adopt their accent:
why? When even in English,
there are still a lot of words you don't know –
wow, so many –
and say you hear a French baby speaking French
you think, "Hey, how'd
that fucking baby get so good?"

Remember that one time,
drunk, when you
told some guy who'd just
gotten back from protesting the Brazilian rainforest,
or something,
"You ain't
shit until you've
read Dante in the original
Spanish,"
and how sober the next morning
you wanted on so many levels
to kick in
your own face?

Or there was that night you biked by
two cops
cuddled together conspiring
cruiser to cruiser
lights off in the parking lot
of the beer store and

knowing you could do nothing,
that there was no number
to call with your speculations,
at home you just speakerphoned saved messages
from your mom and dentist,
and sat
listening in the dark.

Try as you might
you've never been able
to ignore the poetry of trees:
the way they wave
their branches
like rockers to Dokken,
autumn leaves like lighters
swaying blazing in the air –
Alone again, without you.
But whenever people do the wave
you don't do the wave. You
just sit on your hands,
waiting for someone
to score.

Admit it: sometimes you feel like
the only member of a cheerleading team
thrashing about
in a suit of cement.
Not following
but floundering,
while all around you your teammates
fall uncaught crashing to the earth.

So you've been going around lately
with a sort of tightening sensation
behind your ears
that spreads down your neck and

into your throat and holy shit
one of these days your head is
going to split and all the world's
sadness will come pouring out
of your skull lying there in
two pieces like an
egg cracked in half.

You're an egg cracked
in half.

VI

The difference between a tree and a poem
is

this.

"Give me an A."

Autumn Day
(Rainer Maria Rilke)

Lord: it is time. The summer was too huge.
Lay your shadow on the sundial,
and in the meadow give the wind refuge.

Bid the last fruit swell on tree and vine
for two more sun-drenched days;
coaxed to their end, make
from them the sweetest wine.

Whoever has no home now, will never have one.
Whoever is alone, will always be alone,
will stay up nights, read, write long letters
and wander the avenues, up and down,
while the restless leaves are blown.

Acknowledgements

Thanks: Mike and Jon at Snare for their dedication, kindness, and support. Please read Mike's book, *Jack*, and Jon's most recent book, *Stripmalling*.

Thanks: Alex Porco for amazing editorial guidance and encouragement. Please read Alex's books *The Jill Kelly Poems* and *Augustine in Carthage*.

Thanks: Balint Zsako for a stunning cover image. Please visit www.balintzsako.com to see more of Balint's remarkable work.

Thanks: to the Ontario Arts Council for financial assistance.

"The Proper Grammar," "Who's Josh?," "Baseball: A Cricketer's Primer," and "The Fancy Traveller's Guide to Europe" were first published in *Matrix* magazine.

The poems that comprise "Five Very Short Poems About America" were first published as part of a longer series on the website www.elevenbulls.com.

"Explaining Novelty T-Shirts to My Mom" was first published on the website www.mcsweeneys.net.

No grandfathers were harmed in the making of this book.

Thanks.